Love From Two Worlds

A Book of Love Poems

Karlina Dunston

ISBN: 978-1-916596-35-1

Dedication

*To every living soul on
mother earth who has experienced
love and did not have the words
to say how they felt.*

"Is this Love"

The missing of you rearranges my entire thought process. I am concerned I am thinking, I am nosey, I want to be with you. I want to know how are you? Where are you? Who are you with? Are you happy? Are you thinking of me? Do I light the fire in your body where you crave the thought of me? You want to smell my perfume, taste my energy in your belly with my food. Does your heart beat with a beat of missing me? Does the thought of you Never seeing me again disturbs your heart? Will the void be so big and empty that God himself will have to put a handprint in you, to connect you again?

"The Love Only One Knows"

My love for you No one will understand. This love sees past every smell of unpleasantness your body could produce. Any imperfection your skin can show. This love is cosmic and grandiose no one will get it but the stars that the Gods themselves created. This love was created from God and can only be understood without words. Only emotions are responsible for this Great Creation.

"Never Loved"

Love is the Greatest gift that you have not had. You would not believe me if I told you. That love will get in the bed with you every night. In the morning love will be right there to say I love you. When you are worried love will hug your soul, spirit, and physical body. Love will stare you down and tell you don't do that because if you do you will not wear my name properly. And if you do that you have never had me. Love will sneak up on you and jump inside of you from the wind. Love will make you wear it and you will not even know it. Love will make you certain this is it. Love is so Powerful you Never had it because if you did you will Never be the same.

I saw you from 50 meters away my eyes saw you perfectly. The anxiousness of longing for your eyes I was starved. Love had exploded in me. I saw your deprivation of her and my body crave to want to share her with you. I saw you never Tasted the missing of your soulmate gone and then returned. Love you never had her and I made it my mission to implant her inside of your heart. Your heart was closed off like a door with wooden boards and rusty nails and a sign of No Trespassing. I magically and effortless removed all that rubbish and replaced it with every scent that love has and every beautiful flower that love shows. You are a natural experiment of a positive miracle of love.

"Love is Lovely"

There is No place I rather be than in love. She is the most divine force. Love is my comfort zone. I can be inside of her for hours and days. She is beyond intoxicating. The feeling of her is inside not only my entire body, but in every organ in my body. She is in different universes and star systems yet she makes her presence known inside of me and out of me every day. People can smell her on me and they feel her she is incredible the most fabulous, astonishing, invigorating, adulated woman I have ever met and I have not ever seen her only felt her in my body.

"Memories"

I hope you take our love into everyday of your New life. Our memories of each other will always live and not be forgotten they are recorded to the soul akashic records. The New days may feel lonely, but close your eyes and listen to my voice I love you. Remember the way I caressed your hair, prepared your meals, kissed your face, talked love words in your ear. Hold on to my body you know I was something different out of this world. You didn't believe you deserve it. You were wrong the Gods and Goddesses and the universe took a breath and I was the wind they blew out into your life. They showed you that you are worth it to be loved like the world care for you and knew your name. At no time forget the excitement I brought to you when you remember.

"Happy Heart"

True love is butterflies around your whole body in your skin. Happiness that has your heart beating with palpitations. Excitement of the face of value. That is what you mean to me valuable in every sense of the word. No one can compare to the constant emotions of joy in my head, heart stomach, the exciting feeling that I am about to see the greatest person in the whole world in this moment in this life.

Happiness to me is a smile and grin from ear to ear showing all teeth that are able to fit out of one's mouth. The thoughts that are attached to the emotion of seeing you tomorrow is well it is like I don't want to wait. I want to see you Now. My heart and soul is with your heart and soul beating together in the astral plane. Our brains are connected no matter how many miles are in between. Our soul is connected no matter what we think. Too be at work talking to coworkers while my mind is ruminating on the essence of you. The smell of you the smile of you the happiness of you. I wait even though tomorrow seems like 10 years from now.

"Simple Love"

Too wake up every day with a kiss and go to bed with you every night is more than a blessing. The Beauty of God is real and I know it because the overjoyed that I get when you are next to me I know that God is the only explanation. To be this content, happy, excited, grateful, appreciative that I was able to experience you God is the only explanation. Something so beautiful a feeling that cannot be described with human words only Emotions that can be felt in heavenly dimensions because the satisfaction of us is Beyond this world it is out of this dimension and felt in every lifetime.

"Connection"

Our love connection is so strong we can be in different parallel universes and the strength of us will create a dimension where we walk right into each other's life. Like bumping into each other in a coffee shop. An instant look at you and my heart is on fire my body moves on its own. It's like magnets are on every part of my skin because I'm being pulled to you like a rose petal on a strong water current. I don't fight I don't resist I go with the flow back to you.

"Not Sure"

Emptiness lives in me daily love I want I see I can taste I can touch, but can I live it? The breath of hope the eyes of the future. The heart of tomorrow the voice of yes. All of this screams I want it and I can have it. Do I know this and believe it?

"Half Love"

Work, Work, Work towards the love you want to have. Why is it so hard? Why do you have to go through so many ups and downs. So many lies, so many deceptions? Why the one we stuck with the one that is only half the prize? Your heart beats and knows that it is more to the story. You know that your desire burns for more. You were exposed to them. You saw your life what you wanted and how you wanted it. The Love of Your Life Pure Innocent untouched a beautiful statute of Pure Gold Beauty. It feels so Right nothing hurtful has ever touched your lips desire and actions of doing right your blood pumps. To only realize that you are standing with the one who is only half the prize.

"Dimension of Love 1"

Love you have ignited strength to my bones.
Desire you brought out of my soul and spirit.
You helped me reach my higher self in the
Heaven's you gave me a reason to live. You
excited my heart you made tears of tomorrow
flow with True Love. A love that is
experienced from other dimensions that
trickled down to this 3D. My soul has been
touched my DNA activated I know you from
yesterdays and my tomorrows will NEVER be
the same. My ears long to hear your voice
that relax my heart and make my cells smile
my love for you goes through every
dimension there is and finds you. We will
connect again. Different bodies different
languages same souls. My soul will pick you
out of 8 billion people in the world.
Magnetism is inevitable addicted we are to
each other. Talk of this is it one last time

swirls our lips. But our ears are on the same frequency our soul knows that this is incredible and our human emotions cannot control our soul from the others as hard as we try in a circle again we meet to find.

"Unknown Familiar"

My organs move when we talk, they know a familiar sound they recognize the frequency of us. The Body talks and the mind listens we love each other from outer space to inner space, to this place. Like magnets being pulled apart we get cut off, but the invisible strings of life are cemented binding our souls together we don't know this, but our connection is real it's here it's one that can be felt and touched.

"Losing Love of Yesterday"

My heart is being plucked out of my chest and I'm still walking suffocating from the nose down. I can't breathe death of who this person was is dying slowly. I can feel every part of this process it is unbearable. Love is a terrible feeling a Lost like no other not having it is better than going through the pain. Tears of memories fall from my eyes. My heart is literally hurting from pain. I have to kill this person who I am. Coldness is what I am embracing. Nourishing happiness will be turned into sadness of glory of pain.

"Clueless of Cosmic Love"

It is so hard for you to understand me. I need your heart open for your comprehension. Your words need to align with our souls. Your eyes need to see beyond today and tomorrow. Our desires are burning for Each other. But the essence of you stops us from bliss. I don't have all the answers I just have today.

"Love of Surprise"

You came as a pleasant surprise
Who knew my heart would end in a demise
I experienced instant joy, like a child with a new toy

The heavens brought us together with the world in a crazy place.

I was instructed to help you, but I was helping me too.

I am happy to have met you again. You activated my soul in so many ways. The high of us would last for days. My final confession is that this was the hardest lesson. Meeting you lets me know that this is possible for me to have the ultimate connection.

My mind went crazy with the thought of us as a dynamic duo. I had our life planned out with zero doubts.

Then reality sat in that you would just be like a next of kin.

finis (the end)

"Difficult Love"

My heart beats of palpations I fight back the tears I realized that it is over. It is finally over my heart skips beats because the blood is in the moment of when we were in love. My mind and brain are remembering the pain. Saddened my face becomes because the thought of hurting you is not anything I ever wanted to do, but it had to come. Do I be true to you or true to me? The right answer is simple. Love of myself comes first above all. When I can no longer look at you with the desire to split my physical body in half and let you step inside me, I know I must turn and walk away. My body use to want you so bad. Does that mean that love has left me forever?

"Sun Love"

The sun is a new love every day. You can go outside and get kissed by it instantly. The sun's love can be felt without any words. The illumination of its energy kisses you on every part of your skin. The sun is nature and God's love every day. It is present daily and never fails. Love from above to below to me to us to we.

"Don't Recognize"

As I sit here in the car looking at the snow our conversation you just had with me I realize that you don't know me. You don't recognize me. I stand in front of you bare and all showing you all my flaws and love. I love hard it is in my actions it is in my demonstration. You might as well be blind because you can't see me. You can't navigate a love so pure its foreign to you. You don't speak this language of love that I do. The language of my ears hearing what you need and my body goes in nurture mode providing you the support of a lifetime. A task I see so friendly and so innate in me, but you don't recognize me. You will know who I am when I am gone.

"I am Here"

The love of today is stronger than it ever was. The flow of me is on automatic for you. Whatever you need I am there. My body heart and soul all the cells in my body know who you are they want to be assistance to you from the cosmic Mother Nut. The love of me is here tomorrow.

"Love From Growth Within"

I love you and I never met you. You are a complete stranger to me, but you grow within me and I love you. You are part of me and I love you and feel like I cannot do anything right. I want you to have the best crib, best bed, best food, best clothes, best education, best mother, best father. I want you to have the best chance at this thing called life. You are a beautiful soul and I love you. I don't want to mess it up. I want you to have the best be the best and I want of all things to love you the best because you chose me. You chose me to be your mama. You loved me and wanted me. I love you and you will never know how much I do.

"Fear of Love"

Letting go of fear of love. You have to be open like the sky and never close. Your heart must be open to the blue sky the midnight sky. You must be fearless and strong in your thoughts un-wavered by the thought of a broken heart. You must love without reservations you must love without hesitation, you must love without expectations and be open like the blue sky.

"I Want To"

Love of obsession I see you. I see you. I love you so much I want to be inside you. This feeling of love takes a turn of great feeling. I want to protect you. I want to love you. I want you to feel my presence. I want to be all that you need. I want us to be inside each other's body at a quantum level. I want us to experience the universe inside each other. This is not obsession this is completion for me. To feel that you want to give all you have to this person. You want to give everything and if you don't have it. You will go get it. This is Devotion.

"Love Destination"

Love is the final destination of ALL of our lives. We don't even know it, but we all crave the feelings of Love from people we don't know strangers, everyone, anyone, a pet, animal doesn't matter love is the ULTIMATE destination of our lives. We can feel that feeling of completion when we have it. We know this is it. This is my stop the Love Destination.

"Real Love"

I know that real love definition is defined by emotions, feelings, and soul shaking responses from our bodies. Real love really cannot be described, but it doesn't hurt you it makes you feel euphoria for many days to come and is eternal. Real Love is endless through space, time, ether, physical, spirits, souls, and days and nights. It can go on forever.

"Same Love Experience"

Every time I see you it is the first time of Love. I get to experience Love all over again. I look you in your eyes and my soul makes love to you right there in the astral plane. My heart is in love and you feel the same way. It is you it is me it is magical. It is pure love again.

"Definition"

The thought of making you happy and putting a smile on your face is what I do it for. My love for you cannot be fit into a definition of one's thought, but only my thoughts and my definition. I love you presently, now, tomorrow and evermore. Even if I never see you or talk to you again, I will still love you.

"Never Fails"

Love has me keep coming back it is not infatuation, but pure magnetism in the best way. My body gets vibrations of thrills looking at you. Your mouth salivates like a dog when you see me your body cannot control itself. Love is when your body recognizes someone your mind thought was a stranger, but the feeling you get is like old times from a past life. This is liberating it is great, it is good, it is definitely love.

"Missing Love"

Not to love is aberration of human nature. We kept missing each other every month. I love you, you love me, but why didn't it work? Something so simple, but so complex. Love to us must have been so abstruse because we didn't get it right. How can love of one another be chasing the other, only to find nothing, but flaws and failures. Love must have two sides. The people who find it and know what it is and the people who miss it because they can't feel to see it.

"Heart Handling"

I am staring at you in your eyes and I am giving you the greatest task of a lifetime that can alter my future steps. I am trusting you with my delicate heart. The life force of my entire body. This organ pumps blood to every limb and every part of my body. It is so important that you handle it with care and not jab it with a knife or poke it, drop it, kick it or stomp it. If this heart of my mines is not feeling the love, it can stop beating and stop nourishing my whole body and shut down my life. The handling of my heart with love is life to my body.

"Remember Love"

Even when you are nowhere near me, I can smell your body. I remember every hair on your head. I can close my eyes and know the structure of your face. The love I have for you can identify you in pure darkness. I can always find the love of my life. If my life was over, I am sure to see you on the other side because my love is just that real.

"Ownership Love"

You said you waited your whole life for me. The greatest responsibility I had in my life. To be given a gift like this to have the heart and life path of my partner in my hands. I have to get this right the love must be right. The love must be extraordinary, the love must be intense. The love must be gentle, over bearing, overwhelming, and passionate. My way, your way, our way, no you want it your way, I want it my way. I own you I have you. I love you. I don't want to let you go I can't see you with anyone else. You are mines. Love is in you I put it in there and you both belong to me.